Generational Curses

Pastor Brian Gallardo
Copyright © 2018 Brian Gallardo Ministries

Brian Gallardo Ministries
PO Box 3195
Independence, MO 64055
816.503.9586

Copyright © 2018 Brian Gallardo Ministries

All rights reserved solely by the author. No part of this book may be reproduced in any form without the permission of the author.

Unless otherwise indicated, all bible quotations are taken from the King James Version. Some scripture quotations are the author's paraphrase.

Printed in the United States

Book cover designed by:
Staci Dabney Photography
www.sdabneyphoto.com

DEDICATION

I dedicate this book to every child that grew up without loving parents. To every foster child who is lost and confused. I dedicate this book to every broken soul on life's journey, trying to find hope and healing. I dedicate this book to every person who was abused physically, emotionally and sexually. May you find hope and healing on the following pages.

CONTENTS

Foreword

Acknowledgments

Introduction

1 Sin, Trespass, Iniquity

2 Sources Of Curses

3 Transferable

4 The Devil Is A Liar

5 He Is After Your Seed

6 The Spirit Behind It All

7 The Test

8 Acknowledgement

9 Steps To Freedom

FOREWORD

Pastor Brian Gallardo has emerged as a powerful voice to this generation. He is man of great character with an unbridled passion for Jesus. He is an effective communicator whether through preaching or writing. I am honored to call him, friend. I recognize the special grace and incredible gift that is at work in his life.

In this book, "Breaking Generational Curses," Pastor Gallardo tackles the all too familiar issues that plagues so many of our lives. However, his approach is a unique blend of blunt transparency mixed with the compassion which only comes through experience. He not only uncovers the problem; but, helps identify the root of the problem, giving us the opportunity to confront our own roots. Thus, empowering us to live a free life. This book is not for those looking for relief. Rather, it is for those seeking a remedy. Relief is temporary. But, a remedy provides true deliverance and freedom.

All of us have experienced some type of abuse, abandonment, rejection, or tragedy that has opened a door for generational curses to attach themselves to our lives. This book will close those open doors and reveal how to live free.

This is not just a book. This is journey that will take you into wholeness. Pastor Gallardo shares from his own experiences and the work of freedom that has come to his life. Prepare to be provoked and challenged. Prepare to be healed. It's your time to experience the "Breaking of Generational Curses."

Pastor Jonathan Miller
Lead Pastor
New Beginnings Church
Orlando,FL

ACKNOWLEDGMENTS

Thank you to all of the men and women who have given me countless opportunities and chances. I know I would have never become the man I am today had it not been for the following people: My gracious and loving wife, Pastor Jillian Gallardo, my mother Sherry Gallardo, my grandparents, Jack and Mary King. My amazing in-laws Pastor Jeffrey and Barb Becker. Dr. Maurice Hart, Pastor James Hart, Pastor James Bradley, Dr. Rod Parsley, Bishop and Pastor Kathi Pitts. My sister in-law and dear friend, Jenae Starr Becker. Countless spiritual sons and daughters in the faith. Friends and peers who have encouraged me along the way. I see you and I acknowledge you!

INTRODUCTION

Have you ever wondered why you are the way you are? Why you can't stop doing what you do? Why you LOVE the things that you should hate? Why for you, it's "easy" to do things that have always been done the way they have been done in your family, while at the same time you know those things are wrong? Then give me your attention over the following pages of this book as I talk to you about Breaking Generational Curses and familiar spirits. It's a message that I believe is going to help so many in the body of Christ.

Most times, when an author writes about this subject, or a preacher preaches about this subject, folks want to argue about the powers of the supernatural. However, if you are a person of faith, everything about the walk of faith is supernatural. Everything about God and His Word is supernatural. Satan doesn't want this book in your hands. He will try and get you to STOP reading it over the course of time it takes you to read it. Many times, when I preach on this subject, I see demons manifest right during the teaching of the word. Satan doesn't want to move or come out; he doesn't want humanity free.

I am not saying you are demon possessed if you have any of the traits listed in this book (although you may be). However, you may be bound and ***lean toward*** traits that your forefathers just "did." In this book, I'm going to believe with you for total freedom and deliverance from those "traits!"

Exodus 20:4-6 You shall not make for yourself a carved image—any likeness of anything that is in heaven above, or that is in the earth beneath, or that is in the water under the earth; you shall not bow down to them nor serve them. For I, the Lord your God, am a jealous God, ***visiting the iniquity of the fathers upon the children to the third and fourth generations*** *of those who hate Me, but showing mercy to thousands, to those who love Me and keep my commandments.*

The iniquity visits four generations to those who "hate God." I know none of you reading this book hate

God because your freedom is tied to your desire to please the heart of the Father. Many of you have been through some things in life and are frustrated with, or mad at God That doesn't mean you hate God. The blessing is going to flow and the curse is going to be broken.

I am a firm believer that there are some types of bondages: PRAISE, GIVING, CHURCH attendance, BEING in leadership, etc. that simply won't get you to your freedom. Sometimes you have to change the process of your thinking, and the only way that can happen is if you receive anointed TEACHING on the subject matter. Generational curses cannot be broken until you see things a different way. "Strongholds" are the ways we think that are contrary to the Word. Most people think in such ways because they have never seen things differently.

Furthermore, just because you have been shown how to do something by someone you look up to, doesn't mean it's the right thing to do. You could have been taught wrong. If you think wrong is right because you have been taught that way, your thinking is broken. Thus, you have a stronghold operating in your life. Many times, this is seen in families. The good news is – YOU CAN BE FREE!

Galatians 3:13-14 Christ has redeemed us from the curse of the law, having become a curse for us for it is written, "Cursed is everyone who hangs on a tree," that the blessing of Abraham might come upon the Gentiles in Christ Jesus, that we might receive the promise of the Spirit through faith.

He redeemed us so that the blessing given to Abraham might come to the Gentiles. You and I have a right to the blessing through Jesus Christ. It is by faith we are to receive the promise of the spirit.

As you read this book, get some quiet time to allow the Holy Ghost to examine your heart. Allow Him to show you things and speak to your heart. Get a pen and notepad handy to journal your thoughts and allow freedom to ring.

My prayer for you as you are reading this book is simple, yet powerful: *"May the Lord fill your spiritual ears with His word to enable you to hear the Holy Ghost speak deliverance and freedom in the precious name of Jesus."*

I encourage you to decree the following statement, out loud, before you begin: *"I am open to being wrong. I am open to freedom. I am open to walking in the fullness of Jesus. Lord, reveal to me my error that has been passed down from generation to generation and empower me to **lean towards** holiness and repentance in Jesus name."*

Let's dive in…

CHAPTER 1
SIN, TRESPASS, INIQUITY

In Exodus, God speaks to Moses and Moses declares, *"**the iniquities** of the fathers visit generations four times down. But **the blessing** will visit generations to come."* You and I are the "generations to come." We are to partake in the blessing of Abraham. If you're Abraham's seed, you've been grafted into the things of God. Galatians teaches us that Christ **busted the curse** for us by becoming the curse on the cross.

The curse that I want to explain to you is essential for you to understand. The "generational curse" explained in this book is not referring to the "curse" brought upon the earth due to Adam's fall in the garden. That "curse" was broken by our Lord as he hung on a tree two thousand years ago.

"Generational curses" are the traits and dysfunctions in your family that continue from one generation to the next. Many of you are blinded and don't even see the unbiblical traits working in you, because you grew up in a family where wrong was "normal." To you, dysfunction is "normal" because it is just what your family does.

This dysfunctional "normal" in your family has been passed down from generation to generation leading you to think a certain way. Things run through your mind like "it may be wrong but this is just how our family does it" or "that's just how we roll." Now friend, to be free you have acknowledged the fact that something is broken or wrong. You won't see any change come to ANYTHING if you're unwilling to acknowledge that things are broken and or dysfunctional. Just because your family has done things for so many years doesn't make those things right.

There could be a generational curse that has plagued your family many generations back. It could be that what you call normal is not normal according to the biblical standard.

Exodus 20:5 teaches that ***the iniquities*** of the fathers ARE passed down… Your Bible shows three major types of sin. There is **sin,** there's **trespassing,** and then there's **iniquity.** Each one has a different meaning.

SIN means that you miss the mark. Everyone reading this book is going to miss the mark today or this week at some point. No one is perfect, and we all are guilty of missing the mark. Saved or not, how holy you are, how many suits you wear, if you carry a big King James Bible to church-it doesn't matter how holy you think you are; you're going to miss the mark. That sin, you didn't set out to do it, but you did it. You didn't mean for it to happen, but you did it. Or the things you should have done but didn't do them: you didn't read your Bible, you didn't pray, you missed the mark. ALL of us are guilty.

TRESPASS means you knew where the boundaries were, but you went over the mark; did it anyway and didn't care. A good example of a trespass can be seen in 2 Kings 5. Naaman came to the Prophet Elisha and asked him to heal him of leprosy. The Prophet gave Naaman specific instructions pertaining to his healing. Naaman obeyed the instructions and was healed. Naaman wanted to bless the man of God for giving him the instruction of the Lord which ushered in his healing. Elisha refused and wouldn't have any part in that.

2 Kings 5:16 But he said, As the Lord lives, before whom I stand, I will receive nothing.

Naaman departed from Elisha and went his way. Elisha had a servant by the name of Gehazi. He saw the miracle go down and the conversation between Naaman and Elisha. He couldn't believe Elisha would turn down wealth and riches from Naaman. So, he chased Naaman down *(even after Elisha publicly said he didn't want a thing)* and asked for payment. Gehazi trespassed and bold faced lied right to Naaman.

2 Kings 5:21-24 So Gehazi pursued Naaman. When Naaman saw him running after him, he got down from the chariot to meet him, and said, "Is all well?" And he said, "All is well. My master has sent me, saying, 'Indeed, just now two young men of the sons of the prophets have come to me from the mountains of Ephraim. Please give them a talent of silver and two changes of garments.'" So Naaman said, "Please, take two talents." And he urged him, and bound two talents of silver in two bags, with two changes of garments, and handed them to two of his servants; and they carried them on ahead of him. When he came to the citadel, he took them from their hand, and stored them away in the house; then he let the men go, and they departed.

Elisha told Naaman he didn't want a thing. Gehazi was right by his side when that conversation happened. Gehazi knew what his master said to Naaman, yet Gehazi **trespassed** and did the opposite of what was instructed.

INIQUITY is a **SIN** that is continually practiced until it becomes a habit or a way of life; a "lifestyle." Iniquity means when a sin is practiced in your life until that thing ***becomes normal to you***. The Hebrew word for iniquity means ***to bend or "lean towards."*** Your family and my family all bend a certain way; they all have issues and addictions and problems. Every family has "elephants" in the room at our annual family reunions. I'm not talking about narcotic addiction alone-maybe its emotional abuse; they've been that way for generations. Maybe it is a form of manipulation through guilt trips; they've been that way for generations. Maybe your dad's dad left him and your dad left you.

Being fatherless is not normal and that trait can be broken with you! Maybe when you grew up your momma was divorced, your grandpa was divorced, and your great-grandfather was divorced, so for you, divorce is OK and "normal." But in all actuality divorce is anti-God and anti-bible. Now, if there is abuse or infidelity, there are grounds for divorce. I'm referring more to marriages that end because of lust and pride. If you've been divorced, please hear my heart-there should be zero condemnation or shame in your game about your past. You can't change what you have done or gone through. However, you can change your "now" situations and also where you are headed next. I believe in restoration with all my being. I believe in the power to overcome the history of our past. You are now a new creation if you are in Jesus and no longer labeled or known by your past. As a follower of Jesus, you are known by your future in Him. However, for you to get divorced because you don't agree on the mortgage payment is anti-God. That's a dysfunction and a generational iniquity. It is something you lean towards as "okay" simply because you've been raised to **bend** that way. A lie has been taught to you if you've been taught that divorce is "acceptable."

Many times you know a Generational Curse has a hold on a family when it gets into a certain circumstance or a certain environment. If a Generational Curse is operating, it will cause you to want to bend the way your family bends. So, if drinking five shots of whiskey before you go to bed is deemed "normal" because that's what you saw your daddy do growing up, then for you, in your mind, you tend to want to ***bend*** that way. When I am speaking of the word ***bend***, I simply mean it's easy for you to ***lean*** into that type of thinking. If getting your buzz on is okay because your daddy did it to make him "feel better" and fall asleep quicker, then you can ***bend*** that way as well, finding this behavior to be "acceptable." For you to take any mind-altering drug just to feel better and make your emotions get altered because you've seen your parents take a substance to "take the edge off," you are DUPLICATING bondage, and you have a stronghold. Now it is easy for you to think these things are normal because you're **bent** that way. The unfortunate thing is when you have children, your children will see you **bend** that way and then they will think it's "acceptable" for them to **bend** that way too.

Curses are carried out to "the generations to come." From the first generation, second generation, third generation, fourth generation, it then goes on to visit the "generations to come." It is not normal and doesn't have to be what the _____ (put your last name in the blank) family does. Change the order, break the cycle, be different, and BE FREE!

God wants us to put our foot down and stand up strong to the vices that have bound our forefathers. You can do it! You can walk in freedom! Your kids can be free! We're going to break some curses, traits, bends, and cycles today!

When you practice sin, and when you trespass over and over and over and over and over again, it turns into iniquity. It turns into the way you ***bend***. It turns into the vice that becomes a "spiritual DNA." A spiritual DNA in your family is as powerful as the natural DNA. Every family has its own culture or their way of doing things in life. Some family cultures produce productive citizens to the community. Others family cultures do not. Some families think it's acceptable to be in everyone else's business and spread it to everyone they know. Their family is known for gossip. It is the culture of some families to spend more money than they have, and so they are always in a financial crisis. Some family cultures produce men who are jerks to women and abuse their wives physically or emotionally, demeaning and cutting them down. Their culture and way of thinking, produces a cycle of "putting the wife in her place." They like to quote and misuse scripture and give the excuse of "well pastor, my wife is supposed to submit to me." When in all reality, in marriage, we are supposed to submit to each other. That is an unbiblical, abusive mindset. Just because your daddy didn't treat your mom right doesn't mean that way of thinking is right.

Just because you have something displayed in front of you by your parents, doesn't mean that display was right. I believe a wife should submit to her husband, but I also read the rest of the bible. A husband should lay down his life for his wife as Christ laid down His life for the church. We as men should give up our wants and desires and die to our wants to give our families their wants and needs! We as husbands have the bigger responsibility. "Well, as a man, I am supposed to be macho! I am never supposed to cry!" Who told you that? Your daddy? Your dad also abused your mom, never hugged or kissed his kids, and drank every night. Show me a man that will cry in front of his family and I'll show you a man that is probably a good husband and father.

Break the cycle! Break that way of thinking. Break all the unbiblical mindsets. Break the drama. God does not want his children to always be in the middle of a crisis. If your family is crisis centered, break this way of thinking! Your family could and may be wrong. Your family's ways aren't necessarily the right ways. You're not called to live after the culture of your family. You are called to a higher culture, the culture of the Kingdom!

CHAPTER 2

SOURCES OF GENERATIONAL CURSES

Where did these curses come from? Why are they manifesting in the life of my family? In the following moments, I am going to pull the covers back and reveal some of the sources by which Generational Curses come and move upon a family. I do not intend to come off as if I "know it all," but simply as a man who has been freed from multiple generational curses and has seen where many of their sources come from. Allow the Holy Ghost to speak to your heart and show you the sources in your own family's spiritual DNA.

SOURCE #1: WORDS

Job 22:28 you will also declare a thing, And it will be established for you.

Proverbs 18:21 Death and life are in the power of the tongue, And those who love it will eat its fruit.

Words hold power, life, and death. Curses usually come in the form of words. Blessings and/or curses can come out of our mouth. You can tear somebody down or uplift them with your words. When someone compliments you, you feel warm and fuzzy. When someone critiques you who doesn't even know or love you, you feel hurt and angry all because words have power.

Have you ever heard the old saying "sticks and stones may break my bones but words will never hurt me?" That is not true. Words hurt people; words destroy people, words split churches, words split marriages, words break the hearts of children, words bring all kinds of drama. Words can make you lose a job; words can make you go crazy on Facebook, words can do all kinds of stuff.

Thus, as we don't like when others hurt us with their words, we must be careful not to hurt the ones we love by speaking words of death to them. I want you to decree this so your ears can hear it: *"Mouth, you will declare, and you will decree the blessing of the Lord."*

We have got to remove ourselves from the thinking that whatever we say doesn't really matter. We live in a time where we are encouraged to say whatever we feel. Folks boast their feelings and opinions on Facebook and Twitter and act as if it doesn't really matter. We can talk to people any old way, and it doesn't really matter. But friend, the Bible teaches us the very opposite principle. What you say DOES matter. The words that come out of your mouth DO matter! With your speech, you can ruin a family, destroy your destiny, or move a mountain.

As a preacher, I preach to bring life, through my mouth. Pay attention to what you're decreeing over your family. Be careful what you say to your kids. Don't call them stupid, chunky, fat, ugly, dumb, or a a mistake. You are cursing them if you do!

Mark 11:23 "...whosoever shall say **(DECREE)** *unto this mountain 'Be thou removed, and be thou cast into the sea, and shall not doubt in his heart but shall believe that those things which he saith* **(DECREES)***, shall come to pass; he shall have whatsoever he saith.* **(DECREE).**

If you are cursing your marriage by decreeing "this isn't going to work," "I think we should separate," "he is an idiot," or "she has the worst attitude," you are CURSING your marriage and the marriage of your children. Your children are hearing their authority (you) curse your marriage. You are teaching them it is a "normal" thing to talk and act that way in a marriage, and they will bend that way when they get married. Repent and start speaking life. Repent and start speaking the blessing of the Lord over your life, marriage, family, finances, and home.

SOURCE #2: DISOBEDIENCE TO GOD

Deuteronomy 28 is known as the blessing and cursing chapter in your Bible. I really encourage you to read the whole chapter. There are 14 blessings and 54 curses in Deuteronomy 28.

Deuteronomy 28:1-2 Now it shall come to pass, if you diligently obey the voice of the Lord your God, to observe carefully all His commandments which I command you today, that the Lord your God will set you high above all nations of the earth. And all these blessings shall come upon you and overtake you, because you obey the voice of the Lord your God…

This doesn't mean God is cursing you. It does mean, however, that God won't bless you if you don't obey him. It would be like if I told my daughter, "Olivia, the stove is hot, do not touch it." And yet, even though I told her not to, she still wanted to. So, she touches it and gets burned badly. She comes to me crying and says, "Daddy help me I got burned, please take the pain away, please bless me." I can't do anything to help the pain. We cannot live in the blessing of the

Lord and still do things to our pleasing. Blessing flows when we obey the Word, and blessing will not flow if we disobey his Word.

Look at all the blessings attached to obedience in Deuteronomy 28:

* **Exaltation:** You'll be lifted up.
* **Re-productiveness:** What you do or put your hands to will multiply. A lot of people are not productive because they don't obey God. They live how they want to, and do what they want to. They come to church clapping Alleluia on Sunday morning, but there's no obedience in their life.
* **Healthy Bones:** Obedience opens the door to healing.

* **Prosperity and Success**
* **Victory**
* **Authority**
* **Strength and Power**
* **Favor:** You will be the head and not the tail. When I think about being the head and not the tail, I think of a dog. If you are at the head of a dog, that is where the dog makes decisions and where first things come. If you are at the tail of the dog, you will see the last things and have to deal with a whole lot of pooh. You can't walk in disobedience and expect to be blessed; it just doesn't happen that way. God loves you; you're going to end up in heaven probably. But His blessings will not flow. God is for you, He isn't against you.

Generational curses are not an eternity issue all the time. Sometimes, generational curses keep you from experiencing life in the fullness here and now.

Let's look at all the curses attached to disobedience found in Deuteronomy 28:

* **Humiliation**

* **Barrenness:** No fruit in what you do, every time you try to start something new it fails. Marriage fails, a new church fails, new friendship fails, a new project fails. If you're always failing at what you do, it's a sign that there's a curse in operation.

* **Sickness of All Kinds:** Let me interject for a moment, just because you're sick doesn't mean

that there's a curse operating. BUT if you have diabetes, and your daddy had diabetes, and your great-granddaddy had diabetes, something isn't right in your genealogy. It needs to be broken.

* **Poverty and Failure:** is a sign that the curse is operating.
* **Constant Defeat**
* **Helplessness**
* **Beneath and Weak:** You are generally picked last. Generally, on the bottom of the list, no favor to be found. It seems like you always fail at what you start. It could be that a generational curse is operating it needs to be broken.

SOURCE #3: PEOPLE WHO SPEAK ON BEHALF OF GOD

People who speak on behalf of God can release a curse. In other words, a five fold office gift *(Apostle, Prophet, Evangelist, Pastor, Teacher)*, a governing leader, has the authority to release a curse.

Joshua 6:26 Then Joshua charged them at that time, saying, "Cursed be the man before the Lord who rises up and builds this city Jericho; he shall lay its foundation with his firstborn, and with his youngest he shall set up its gates."

Joshua had just defeated Jericho. Jericho represents to us hindrances that keep us from advancing our purpose. Five hundred years later, King Ahab is in leadership as the king of Israel. A gentleman in 1

Kings 16:34 tries to rebuild Jericho. In Ahab's time, he allowed Hiel to rebuild Jericho. He laid its foundation at the cost of his firstborn son, Abiram, and he set up its gates at the cost of his youngest son, Segub. This followed the word of the Lord spoken (a curse that was spoken) by Joshua, son of Nun.

Joshua spoke a curse that took five hundred years to manifest. Jericho, in your Bible, has never been a good place since Joshua released that curse. Speed up several hundred years later, and you see Jesus came on the scene, and the Bible said Jesus began to talk about Jericho. He said a certain man (the Good Samaritan story) was on his way to Jericho. Jericho was like the modern-day Las Vegas or Amsterdam. Anything you could ever want you could find in Jericho, for Jericho was the sin capital of that region.

Jericho had a curse pronounced on it long ago by Joshua, and still, we saw it manifesting during the time of Jesus.

Let's look into another example:

2 Kings 2:23-24 he (Elisha) was going up the road, some youths came from the city and mocked him, and said to him, "Go up, you baldhead! Go up, you baldhead!" So he turned around and looked at them, and pronounced a curse on them in the name of the Lord. And two female bears came out of the woods and mauled forty-two of the youths.

The Bible said that Elisha looked at these teenagers and *cursed* them. Two bears came up out the woods and mauled them to death.

God ordained governing office gifts to have the authority to speak a curse over things and people that oppose God's way.

SOURCE #4: RELATIONAL AUTHORITY

Relational authority refers to people who are in your life who possess authority over you in some regard. They have the power to curse or bless you. That's why it's important who you're submitted to. If you were to go to a church and the pastor wasn't submitted to another pastor, I would tell you to run and find a pastor who was submitted to spiritual authority. I don't think any person, in authority, in the Kingdom has the right to be on his/her own without being under spiritual covering. I wouldn't submit to a leader who wasn't submitted to somebody. Here are some examples of this found in scripture:

HUSBANDS

Biblically, the husband is to be over his wife. It doesn't mean they are to lord and dictate them, or to micromanage them. God set it up for the husband to be the leader of the home. So, husbands, we've got a greater responsibility than what we realize. It's our job to empower our wife and help her get into the destiny that God has called her to. If we're always putting our wife down, always beating her up in her mind, telling her she's not good enough, "why can't you be as pretty as so-and-so" or "you need to lose a few pounds" etc… Guys, as the relational authority, we should be empowering our wives, we should be blessing our wives, and we should be encouraging our ladies. Men, we should make our wives feel like the queens they are! They ought to feel like princesses around us. Because you're over them, you can bless them or curse them. You can make them wither or bloom. I'm old-fashioned; I believe you ought to still open the door for your lady. I believe as the man, we should empower and not curse or oppress our wife.

PARENTS

Parents, you have relational authority over your children. It's important that you speak blessings to your kids. You'll either ruin them or bless them by the words that come out of your mouth, or by the things you display in front of them. You're supposed to take what the bible says and empower your children. What kind of TV shows do you watch in front of them? While sitting with them, what do you put before their impressionable eyes? What kind of songs or music do you allow into their ears and minds? Are you blessing them or cursing them?

CHILDREN

If you're 5 or 25, and your mom and dad are still alive, you should honor them. If you're dishonoring them, you are cursing yourself.

Exodus 20:12 Honor your father and your mother, that your days may be long upon the land which the Lord your God is giving you.

This isn't talking about little kids; this is talking to all of us. If you have a mom and dad and you dishonor them, your life will be shortened.

A long time ago, I was a youth pastor preaching at a youth conference telling my testimony. I was telling a group of amazing students about my father. I called him a chump on the platform because he abandoned his kids. The Holy Spirit apprehended me when I was preaching and said: "don't you ever speak of your dad that way again." So I went back to the hotel, and I knew the Holy Spirit was wanting to speak to me and he said: "do you want to live long?" I said, "yes sir." He said "don't you ever dishonor your father like that again." I said "but he was wrong." He said, "and so are you." He asked me, "Do you want your kids dishonoring you?" I said "no sir," He said, "don't you ever dishonor your dad like that again." His blessing and covenant both work regardless. Whether you like it or not, it will work. Whether you do or don't agree with it, it will work. Relational authority in the home is strong. It is imperative we break the cycle and begin to bless each other Husbands, Parents, and Children.

<u>TEACHERS</u>

Another example of relational authority can be found in what teachers say about their students. A gentleman in my church came up to me one day and said "Pastor, this word is so strong that you're teaching us on generational curses. I remember when I was a little kid, and my mom and dad went to a parent-teacher conference. My mom and dad came home, and I said 'how did the conference go?' they said 'well, it didn't go very good; your teacher said you're lazy.'" He added, "you know pastor, that's one of the things that always hindered me all my life; even up till this day, I'm still trying to defeat it." I laid my hands on him, and I said: "that lie is broken and that curse is removed in Jesus' name."

When an authority figure announces things over those under them, it can both damage and curse them.

SOURCE #5: YOUR FATHER

Fathers can curse a son or a daughter. Dads can break the spirit of a child and embitter them. Dads, it is very imperative that you speak the blessing of the Lord over your children. If you messed up and have said and or done things to your kids that messed them up, apologize to them. Apologize to them for the things you've spoken or done to them; things that have caused them and hindered them. Fatherlessness is an epidemic in our country. If you have abandoned your children, you've cursed them. You can agree with me; if you grew up without your dad, it probably still messes with you as an adult. It still messes with me every once in a while. Father's Day isn't always the best for me. There have been multiple occasions like holidays and birthdays where I wished my dad was around. When a father leaves his family, the children become confused with their purpose. A father is supposed to help shape his children. Fathers are supposed to give confidence to their children and form them into the people God is calling them to be. He is to set boundaries and protect them from harm and struggle. He is a destiny and future giver. He is to display good traits in front of his daughter to give her things to look for in a future husband. He is to display good traits in front of his son to give him an example of what a good man looks like. When a dad abandons and walks out on his kids, there's a gap and a hole that only a father can fill. Thus, if you have left your children, dads, you've cursed them. You need to get right and go back to them and heal them.

I was preaching at a different church one time, and the Lord had me do something I've never done in the past. I was standing at a pulpit and the Holy Spirit spoke to me, "stop preaching, go over and tell the pastor he needs to make things right with his children because he walked out on them." I didn't want to tell him that one bit! But because I fear God over man, I walked over to him, put my microphone down and whispered what the Holy Ghost spoke to me. He was so angry that I never heard from him again. He eventually lost his church, his marriage and went mad.

Obedience equals blessing, and disobedience equals cursing. Dads, you've got the power to bless your kids. If you have messed fatherhood up, put this book down and go to your children and make it right. If you walked out on your kids, reverse the curse. Humble yourself, tell them you're sorry for walking out on them, and own it.

The bible does not say it's the sins of the mothers that are passed down; but it's the iniquities of the <u>Father</u> that's passed down.

Dads, it's important your kids see you come to church, it's important your kids see you pray, it's important that your kids see you read the Bible. Your role as the father in the home is extremely important for the health of your child. Dads, God's going to hold us accountable for how we lead our family.

Matthew 18:6 Whoever causes one of these little ones who believe in Me to sin, it would be better for him if a millstone were hung around his neck, and he were drowned in the depth of the sea.

Colossians 3:21 Fathers, provoke not your children to anger, lest they be discouraged.

I don't know about you guys, but I have failed as a dad before. I've said things that I had to retract and tell Olivia (my daughter) "honey, daddy is so sorry, I said that when I was upset, please forgive me." We have the power to form and shape our children. A little girl needs her daddy to love them. Make your kids feel confident to be who God has called them to be. It's alright if they are not loud; celebrate their shyness. It doesn't matter if they're not shy; celebrate their loudness. I've learned that generally when a parent has a problem with one of their kids' traits, that kid is acting in a way that is exactly like their parent.

Find something you like about them and celebrate them. Stop picking out what you don't like about them. You magnify whatever you say and decree over them.

Proverbs 13:22: A good man leaves an inheritance to his children's children.

This isn't referring to money alone. This is referring to spiritual genealogy as well. If you are a good man, you're going to speak life into your children and leave them a Godly legacy.

SOURCE #6: SELF-IMPOSED CURSES

In Genesis 27, Rebecca said: "what good is my life to me." Don't heap curses on yourself. Saying things like "I am going to die, I just know it," "I am so stupid," "I will never get it right," "I am a horrible person," "My marriage will never be good," etc…

When we say things like Rebecca said in Genesis, i.e., "I am so weary of my life," "what good is my life to me anyway?" "I'm of no use," "I'm of no good," it's like poor Charlie Brown saying "nobody loves me," "nobody wants me." You are literally cursing yourself.

It's easy to talk about how bad we have it, but we're cursing ourselves when we do. Somebody loves you! Stop saying you're not valuable, worthless, nobody cares about you, nobody would notice if you're gone, nobody will notice if you took a whole bottle of Tylenol PM, *"what is my life to me?"!!!* Stop it! There are people that want you, love you, need you, want to see you, be around you; stop cursing yourself. You're literally inviting a spirit of death; you're invoking death upon yourself. Blessing and cursing can be self-imposed.

SOURCE #7: UNSCRIPTURAL COVENANTS

If you're in this category or you know someone who may be, please don't think that I'm pronouncing a curse over you or anything of that nature. But there's a group of guys in our country called the Freemasons. There was a book released in the 50's called "The

Darkness Visible," and it exposes the rites, ceremonial practices, and things the Freemasons indulged in. According to that book, when you become a Mason you've got to pronounce a curse over yourself. The curse goes like this, "If I tell the secrets of the Freemasons, May they cut my tongue out, cut my arm off, and throw it over my right shoulder."

They also practice idolatry. In the "32nd royal arch degree" *(a level of their fellowship)* they worship a false god. This god is a mixture of three words: 1) Jehovah 2) Baal 3) Osiris.

Jehovah is the ultimate God, the God I worship, Baal is what God cursed when Jezebel was in leadership, and Osiris was another god of agriculture that some worshiped in the Old Testament, to which God cursed. Freemasons gather and worship our God mixed with false gods which were cursed and condemned by God (Jehovah).

When you make covenants with those who worship false gods, you are literally making covenants with their false gods. When you make covenants with those whose gods are foreign, you are invoking a curse upon yourself. The same type of thing is seen when people partake in reading horoscopes.

SOURCE #8: TRIBAL PRACTICES

Be careful what you open yourself up to.

Deuteronomy 7:26 Nor shall you bring an abomination into your house, lest you be doomed to destruction like it. You shall utterly detest it and utterly abhor it, for it is an accursed thing.

Anything that advertises sorcery or worship to any other deity other than God should be taken out of your house. We ought not to have superstitious stuff in our house. We should not pray to candles when we can pray to Jesus. We should not pray to a crucifix when we can pray to the one who hung on it. If you have a Ouija board in your house, get it out. I wouldn't listen to music that said anything in a derogatory or demeaning way about our God, the real Jehovah, or stood against what God stands for and vice versa.

Get rid of all religious candles, Buddha statues, dark African artwork, and tarot cards. Get them out of your house and out of your life. Stop reading them, stop playing with them and stop allowing it to come through your TV as you watch and are entertained by them. All forms of superstition should be removed. It's a foreign object, and it's forbidden. There's only one way that's right; God's Way.

SOURCES OF GENERATIONAL CURSES

* Words
* Disobedience to God
* People who speak on God's behalf

* People with relational authority over your life
* Self-imposed curses
* Unscriptural covenants
* Tribal practices
* False gods
* Foreign objects

CHAPTER 3
TRANSFERABLE

Iniquity is transferable. When a father and a mother don't go to church, their kids only have a 4.6% chance of being churched. If a mom and dad do not value the house of God, neither will their children. Parents have the power to transfer traits onto their children.

As a pastor, I see it all the time. I see parents drop their kids off at church and yet the parents don't come with them. Then the child becomes a teenager and has zero desire to come to church. The parent calls the church office and wants to ask us questions about why their child doesn't want to come to church any longer. If it isn't important to you as a parent, it won't be important to your child. They are becoming who and what you are.

Generational traits and curses are transferable. You've got to be careful about what you say to your children and what you do in front of them. Our dysfunctional traits as parents communicate to our children that dysfunction is "normal."

If you get in the car after church and critique every little thing your pastor does, don't expect your child to respect and honor the House of the Lord. It has been said, next to the president of the United States, pastoring a church is the hardest job in America. Instead of critiquing your pastor in front of your child, let your child see and hear you pray for them and bless them. If your child sees you bless and pray for the man of God, they will want to stay close to one. Who knows, they may even want to become one when they grow older. Cursing and blessing can be transferable!

People generally critique what they don't know much about. You wouldn't do as good of a job at pastoring your church as your pastor does. If you could, God would have given you the task. Could you deal with crazy people, getting nasty emails, and having your family threatened? People that take but do not give? Giving yourself and your family to a group of people that end up betraying you, or slamming you on social media? You can't depend on everybody as a pastor; you don't know who's going to be there half the time. Folks will praise you on a Sunday and shout "crucify" on a Friday. No one generally sees the pain a pastor goes through, but folks want to judge the glory they come into. Pastoring people is one of the hardest jobs in the world! I am not complaining because I love what I am called to do, but don't critique what you don't understand in front of your kids, and then wonder why they don't want to participate in what you critique.

When your kids hear you get in the car and start criticizing everything that happened at church, you're transferring a critical spirit onto them. I know you're probably wondering, "why are you pushing this point about the church so much?" American millennials think that if they go to church once a month, they are faithful church attendees. There isn't much honor in the house of God today because a generation of yesterday pushed a dishonoring trait upon them concerning the house of God. Someone has got to rise up, speak up, and break it!

You may think you're slick and going undetected, closet drinking and closet smoking, but your kids are not stupid. They can smell it on your breath. They can see it in your eyes. Don't freak out at them if they tell you at 16 that they are now smoking and drinking. Monkey see monkey do. What you're putting before them is communicating "in this family 'THIS' is normal," when in all reality it is bent and bondage.

What is dysfunctional in your family becomes normal to your children. What the Bible calls off, sin and odd, a dysfunctional family calls normal. To be free from generational curses you must acknowledge and agree with what the Bible calls dysfunction, sin and bondage.

If you live in a family culture that fights all the time, throws stuff, cusses each other out because you didn't get your way, your kids will be bent and lean towards iniquity. Life, wealth, joy, entertainment, and vacations are all a normal biblical standard to have in the home. Chaos, drama, poverty, lies, confusion, and unhappiness are not.

Just like the curse is transferable, so also is the blessing! Deposit faith, transfer a prayer lifestyle, transfer a home filled with joy. Let your kids see what it looks like to have a marriage where two people laugh and have fun in life. Show them what righteousness looks like. Show them that when everybody else is "doing _____" (fill in the blank), Dad and Mom are not, nor will be. Show them, in lifestyle, that you are not going to pass an iniquity onto them. Show them what holiness looks like. Show them, fathers, how a daddy prays for his wife and kids. Let them see you be kind to their mom and empower her.

The curse is transferable; the blessing is transferable! Just like you can transfer the curse, you can transfer the blessing.

Poverty is transferable. Take a kid that's raised in poverty; poverty is what he knows when he is grown unless it's broken.

Addiction is transferable. Take a kid raised in addiction; addiction is what he knows when he is grown unless it is broken.

This is not to say, just because your parents were addicted that it is now okay or meant for you to be addicted too. I am not endorsing the "right" to play a victim card. I am simply saying that what you are doing in front of your kids is producing seed that will affect their future.

Sexual promiscuity is transferable. You see a mom dressing extremely promiscuous; don't expect her daughters to dress modestly. If a dad encourages his sons to look at women in a sexualized way, don't expect the same boys to be sexually pure. That's going to be the culture of normalcy for the young boy growing up.

If a dad is lazy and never works, and sits around all day, that father is cursing his kids and paralyzing their future. (Not talking about people who are disabled-I'm referring to a man that ***won't*** work.)

Divorce, overspending, overeating and financial mismanagement go from generation to generation. If you don't have the money to spend a thousand dollars on your children for Christmas, you are cursing your kids by showing them it's okay to go into debt and spend what you don't have. We don't buy big Christmas gifts in our home if we can't afford it. We are not raising our child to think it is functional to live above our means. Everything I'm writing to you is based out of things that I've broken in my life. You have got to break them too, and the good thing is you can.

When my wife and I first got married, we hired a realtor to sell our first home. The particular realtor I hired seemed to be professional and good at what he did. My grandfather asked me what my realtor's name was. My grandfather had done a lot of business in the city and was familiar with a lot of people. When I told him the last name of the realtor that I hired, he said "uh-oh, that's not a good name. 'Those people' are known to do dirty business."

Every family is known for their traits and character flaws. Those traits are passed down from one generation to the next. If I said the name "Hatfield" you would say "McCoy." The Hatfields and

McCoys remind us of a Jerry Springer episode. Two families for generations, who fought each other, hated each other, stole from each other, and eventually killed each other. In 2002, a peace treaty was signed between the two families. It took a hundred and thirty-eight years of generational drama for no reason. Generational curses are passed from fathers to sons, from sons to sons to sons to sons because curses are transferable.

If you take a child and raise him up in an impoverished environment, that child doesn't have much of a chance to become successful unless that child breaks it in his mind. You take a child that was born into a home where the mom and dad got divorced at a very young age, and all that child has ever known is to see mom struggle, see mom broke, see mom hurt, and see mom abused by every man that says he loves her. That child will see his mom taken advantage of by men who just want something from her because dad is out of the picture. To that child, that type of behavior is normal until it breaks in the mind of that child. How can it break? *(We will learn more about this later on in this book).*

Overspending, substance, abuse, dropping out of high school, lack of education… Break them curses! A "better than you" spirit, a holier than thou attitude, that's a curse. You're taking a God complex for yourself and teaching your kids that you're God. Domestic violence and anger transfers until somebody rises to acknowledge them, see it, and then breaks it. Repeat this after me, ***"I acknowledge that everything I've been taught is not necessarily biblical, truth, or right."***

When you practice these things in front of your children, you teach them to bend toward that way.

Many of you who are reading this are reaping a harvest in your life for something you never sowed for. You saw dysfunction growing up, and that dysfunction got implanted in you. So now you're reaping a harvest of what your parents sowed into your thought process as "normal." The reason it's important for you to break it is that you don't want to sow that into your children.

It will go from one generation to another generation and repeat the cycle; somebody has got to break it!

CHAPTER 4
THE DEVIL IS A LIAR

*John 8:44 You are of your father the devil, and the desires of your father you want to do. He was a murderer from the beginning, and does not stand in the truth, because **there is no truth in him**. When he speaks a lie, he speaks from his own resources, for **he is a liar** and the father of it.*

Once you get free, expect to hear a lot of "TRASH TALK" from the enemy. He loves to paint a false reality in your mind. You will hear things like "oh you're not free" or "you are still messed up" or "you will always repeat the cycle." The devil is a liar! He will never celebrate a win in your life. He and his demons want you trapped, broken and depressed, but as the young people say, "Not today Satan! Not today!"

Demon powers are real. The night that I prepared the message that birthed this book, I went to bed early. At 3:00 AM a demon came into my bedroom and started shaking me; he spoke audibly to me saying, "You will not evict me. I represent generational bondage, and you will not speak this message and free the people." I woke up, and grabbed my wife, and we started walking through our house pleading the blood of Jesus over our daughter, over our marriage, over our stuff, over our church, and over our city, and then I started laughing. You may ask "why did you laugh?" I got excited because everything that comes out of the mouth of a demon is a LIE. He cannot tell the truth. If his lips are moving, he is lying. I started laughing because he was speaking the opposite of what was true. If he told me people would not be freed and he was not going to be evicted… THEN THAT IS THE OPPOSITE OF WHAT WAS AND IS GOING TO HAPPEN! If he is lying to you today and telling you that you will "never be free" from the curses passed down to you, you should shout and give God audible praise because he just lied to you!

Satan (and every demon) is a liar! If he tells you that you're going to get a sickness, you're ***not*** going to get it.

If he tells you he's going to do something and harm you, he *isn't* going to do it. If he tells you that you're not going to do something that you feel God called you to, you *are* going to do it. The only way you will fail is if you believe his lies!

*Mark 16:15-17 And He said to them, "Go into all the world and preach the gospel to every creature. He who believes and is baptized will be saved; but he who does not believe will be condemned. And these signs will follow those who believe: In My name **they will cast out** demons…*

*Luke 10:19 Behold, I give you the authority to trample on serpents and scorpions, and **over all** the power of the enemy, and nothing shall by any means hurt you.*

YOU have the authority to drive satan out! Drive him out of your mind! Drive him out of your thoughts. Drive him out of your home. He only has authority to stay if you do nothing! He cannot stay, his demons cannot stay, his curses cannot stay, they are all coming out. They MUST move! They have been evicted!

DECREE THIS OUT LOUD:
"Devil, you've got to go in the name of Jesus."

Talk to him like a junkyard dog! You can have the victory over him! Mark 16:15-17 and Luke 10:19 are eviction papers given to us legally by governing authority, and satan has got to go!

Somebody asked me about the encounter I had in the middle of the night and said: "were you afraid when that demon came into your room?" No, I was not scared one bit. I was mad! I wasn't afraid because greater is he who's in me than he who's in the world. I know who I am in Jesus, and what I know about the enemy is that he's got to go!

You have authority in Jesus' Name according to Luke 10:19! Satan has got to go. He is going to be evicted! He will not and cannot stay!

CHAPTER 5

SATAN IS AFTER THE SEED

Deuteronomy 30:19 I have set before you life and death, blessing and cursing; therefore choose life, that both you and your descendants may live…

The enemy isn't after just you; the enemy is after your kids. The enemy is always after the seed. He wants to bind you and the descendants to come.

Galatians 6:7 Do not be deceived, God is not mocked; for whatever a man sows, that he will also reap.

If you sow a seed, you will reap a harvest. If you don't sow a seed, you will reap nothing. The enemy isn't after the harvest; he is after the seed. If he can mess the seed up, he can mess the future up. Satan wants to mess up your children (your seed), so the curse keeps on going to rob the future of the blessing. Satan wants the curse to spoil your children (your seed), so the curse ruins what's ahead of them (the harvest). But Jesus is the game changer, the chain breaker, and the curse blocker. He will empower you to rise above and be free so your children (your seed) become productive and successful in this life; walking into their full potential (harvest).

God wants to bless your seed. The blessing is bigger than the curse. The word blessing is mentioned over 600 times in the bible. The word curse is mentioned about half as many times, in some formal fashion.

The blessing is bigger! You and I both want our kids to have bigger! We both want our kids to take on the traits of the blessing more than we want them to take on our family traits. We want our kids to be more like Jesus and less like us!

Both blessing and cursing are vehicles of supernatural power. Take the blessing off of something and see if it works. Put the cursing on something and see how you do. They are vehicles of supernatural power, allowing us to walk in victory or live in defeat.

Some of you think in life you always fail because it's just what you do. No, you always fail because there's a curse that has been passed down and you need to break it.

A generational curse is transferable until somebody steps up and breaks it.

CHAPTER 6

THERE IS A SPIRIT BEHIND IT

Curses are biblically defined much like a blessing. You have to understand that the blessing of the Lord and the curses of the enemy are both supernatural. It's a spiritual thing. You and I are either walking or living a dysfunctional spiritual life or a functional spiritual life.

Abraham was given instructions for the generations to come, that there would be a powerful blessing tied to his descendants. In the Book of Exodus, we see Moses rise. Moses goes into Pharaoh's house and says "Let God's people go." Pharaoh was holding them in captivity as slaves but eventually allows them to leave. The children of Israel then wander in the wilderness for four decades. As they were wandering around, the Bible tells us that there was this guy named Korah who was basically anointed to be the janitor in the tabernacle. He would go in, make sure the curtains were dusted, that everything was clean, and in its place. Korah became prideful in his heart and puffed up. He began to think "I can do what Moses does" and "I want to be a priest in the Lord's temple." The problem was found in that God didn't give instructions for Korah to be the priest. So the Bible says that Korah caused a revolt and two hundred and fifty of the children of Israel stood against Moses and sided with him (Korah). God told Moses "Don't you worry about Korah; I am going to take care of Korah and those who follow him." God told Moses to assemble and gather his people. The children of Israel assembled and came together. Moses stood on the one side and said to all of those with Korah "I want you who are with Korah to stand over there and all of those that are with me, I want you to stand over here and we will see who God honors." The Bible says that Korah gathered two hundred and fifty of his people and they stood together in a circle. Some of Korah's natural sons and decedents went and stood over by Moses. The Bible said that the earth opened up and swallowed Korah and all those who were by his side. However, those by Moses' side were all spared.

Here's what's so awesome. While all that was going on, Korah's natural sons and grandsons, his bloodline, showed up standing next to Moses. They said in their heart, Daddy you are wrong, I respect you, I love you, but you are wrong to criticize leadership. So, the curse and the cycle were broken that day upon the descendants of Korah. The sons of Korah then show up decades later ministering in the temple during the reigns of David and Solomon. They weren't janitors anymore; they were worshippers. That's pretty awesome. The sons of Korah broke a generational curse of rebellion. God even used them to write some of the Psalms.

Psalm 42:1 As the deer pants for the water brooks, So pants my soul for You,

O God.

That's accredited to sons of Korah because they broke the curse and walked into the blessing.

I have done my best to explain, as best as I could, and have allowed the Holy Spirit to speak through me on these pages that generational curses are real and powerful. I also did my best to show you and teach you that you can be free! In the following chapter you will be given a test to see if there are traits you ***bend*** or ***lean*** toward.

CHAPTER 7

THE TEST

I want to encourage you, as you take the test below, not to go on a witch hunt. This test is a tool to see if a generational curse is working against your life. If only one of these is manifesting in your life, this is probably just an area you need to work on but don't freak out.

Unfortunately, when talking about spiritual things, some people get all goofy, and they tilt the wrong way, getting overly spiritual. That's not what I want you to do. I'm bringing awareness to you so you know how to fight against traits and bends that have been passed down to you. The question to ask yourself as you take this test is "do I have this particular thing, constantly manifesting in my life? Is it and has it been an issue in my parents' life, and in generations before me?"

How do I know if a generational curse is working against me?

1. DO YOU CONSTANTLY FAIL?

Do you see in your life, and in the lives of past generations, constant attempts without success? Every business your family tries to start can't seem to succeed. Your family goes to church after church and only stays for a few months. Do people in your family get married, yet they fail at it and don't stay in the marriage? Or maybe your family hasn't ever been able to keep friends for very long; they fail in relationship after relationship. It could be because a generational curse is operating and needs to be broken.

2. IS THERE A HISTORY OF UNTIMELY DEATHS AND SUICIDES? ARE THERE MANY CASES IN YOUR FAMILY OF PEOPLE WHO HAVE DIED PREMATURELY?

It could be that a generational curse is operating and needs to be broken.

3. DO YOU EXHIBIT A HIGH LEVEL OF ANGER?

Ripping the doors off the hinges, punching holes in the wall, road rage, screaming at your spouse and kids with the constant excuse of "I can't stop or calm down," Throwing people through walls, turning green and allowing the "HULK" to come out? I'm referring to a spirit of anger that is seen in many of your family members and is familiar with your family and manifests through you.

4. DO YOU HAVE A HIGH RECORD OF ACCIDENTS THAT ARE UNUSUAL IN NATURE?

I'm not talking about the car wreck you got in last month. I'm talking about everything just seems to break around you. You hear people say all the time concerning you "don't touch it, knowing you you'll break it." If so a generational curse may be operating and you need to break the cycle.

5. DO YOU HAVE A HISTORY OF ABUSE PHYSICALLY, EMOTIONALLY OR SEXUALLY IN YOUR FAMILY?

Is abuse something your family sweeps under the rug? Were you abused by an uncle who was abused by his father? If so the abuse stops today and the cycle is broken in the name of Jesus!

6. IS THERE A HISTORY OF CHRONIC ILLNESS?

Do you see the cycles from generations before you and currently of: repeated colds, long-term generational health problems, your mom died from it, your grandma died from it, your great grandma died from it. Do you deal with weight the way your mom deals with weight and your great grandma dealt with weight?

Are there generational health problems? If so, you need to denounce those things.

My uncle died from diabetes. Diabetes runs on my dad's side of the family, and I am not going to eat myself into sickness. I'm going to manage what I eat, and at the same time apply the spiritual principles of confessing the blessing and rejecting the curse. I know many of you struggle with health and weight, so please hear my heart. I am not trying to beat you up or make you feel bad about your weight. I'm simply trying to help you and bring you into truth. To come against a lie that's been shared with you, to help you come into freedom! You can and will be free from the health curses that have been passed down generationally.

7. DOES YOUR FAMILY HAVE A HISTORY OF MENTAL ILLNESS THAT HAS PROGRESSED THROUGH GENERATIONS?

Meaning your grandpa seemed to be depressed more than not. Your dad was diagnosed as being bipolar, and the doctors are now trying to diagnose you with bipolar schizophrenia. That's progressing. It's gaining momentum from one generation to the next. It is a generational curse that needs to be broken. But the good news is, you can be free!

8. DO YOU EXHIBIT ANY OF THE BEHAVIORS LISTED BELOW?

These are some signs that a generational curse is working:

- You're a control freak trying to control everybody and every situation.
- Are you generally in other people's business and other peoples affairs? Do you have a hard time minding your own business?
- Do you generally try to make others do what you want them to do, and if they don't do it, you manipulate through guilt trips and pity parties?

- Are you manipulative with friends, pastors, and spouses to get what you want?
- Do you have an addictive personality?
- Are you extremely codependent? Sometimes codependency is good in relationships. You can't have a good marriage without some amount of codependency. But it should not be the main thing you operate through. You can do life by yourself; you can be independent. If you are single, you don't need a person to complete you. Jesus should be your all and all and will fill you with FULLNESS of life.
- Are you a person who holds onto everything and cannot

forgive anyone? The power of Un-forgiveness gives birth to depression. A lot of you can't get healed because you won't let stuff go. Jesus said in *Matthew 6:15 But if you do not forgive men their trespasses, neither will your Father forgive your trespasses.* Again, please hear my heart. Many of you have been abused sexually, mentally and physically. There is no way you can forgive the one who hurt you. I want to agree with you. You cannot forgive them without the help of Jesus. You see, the grace of God will enable you and empower you to do what you cannot do on your own. You can't forgive them but if you ask the Holy Spirit to

empower you, He will. He wants to help you so you can be healed and be made whole.
- Social Isolation. If you don't have friends, your mom didn't have friends; your Dad didn't have friends, there's a generational curse and cycle that is being passed to you. God wants you to have friends. "Well, pastor, I think It's okay to have friends, but I just can't trust anybody." You won't have any friends if that is the way you think. People can't trust you with that attitude. That's why they don't want to be your friend. Break that way of thinking! Break the cycle! Break the curse! We need each other. We are stronger together! Don't think

it "normal" to live on an island all by your self. God never intended it to be that way. If you want friends then show yourself friendly. No one is born with social skills; they are learned behaviors. Pick up a book on relationships and empower yourself to break the curse.

You have taken the test. You have discovered many of these things operating in your life. Now, what? Now it is time to learn how to be free and stay that way.

CHAPTER 8
ACKNOWLEDGEMENT

Acknowledgment is the very first step to freedom. You will never change what you won't admit or own up to. You can't change it in your mind until you acknowledge that it is wrong. Things begin to change when you first acknowledge them in your mind. In time, as your mind changes, so will everything else. You need to be determined that you are going to make a change.

I decided to spend a whole chapter talking about the first step to your freedom. If you cannot admit and own traits from past generations, you will never get free. I say to you to acknowledge the decree below and speak it out loud so your ears can hear it. Remember the Word teaches us that Faith comes by hearing… (Romans 10:17).

DECREE: *"As for me and my house we're going to serve the Lord, I honor my mom, dad, grandparents and those who made a way in past generations. I honor everything they did for me growing up. But as for me and my house, I am doing it God's Way. Period! I am breaking the curse; it stops here; the cycle is over. I have to break it to empower those to come after me. I denounce all generational curses and allow freedom to flow in and through me."*

At some point, the sons of Korah had an eye-opening moment. Their eyes opened to see that what was **bending** in their family wasn't right. A generational curse comes when a family practices sin until that sin becomes their way. Another definition of that would be a stronghold. The word "stronghold" can be defined as ***the way that one thinks***. If you think a certain way is normal, but that way is not biblical, acknowledge it then pray for God to give you strength to overcome it.

Let's be honest, growing up for 18 years under the same roof, learning dysfunctional systems can be a challenge when it is time to break bad thinking. You won't be able to break it in one book read. You can't break it listening to one message or reading one book. Like a screw driven deep into wood, some things must be backed out and undone. What I'm doing right now is opening the seal so you can see that not everything you think is biblical. Household drama, perversion, being a busybody, always wanting medicine, etc. needs to be confessed to Jesus and acknowledged from your lips.

Freedom comes from confessing the sin and confessing the Word that is contrary to what you call normal. How many scriptures have you read today? How many times I wish some of you would pray and read scripture as much as you click the like button on social media. If you want to be free, get your face out of Facebook and get your face into His book. Start confessing His word over your life concerning areas that you struggle with and watch the Word work!

Generational curses are

transferable. When you go to a doctor they give you a piece of paper to fill out. This paper is filled with questions about your mom and dad. They ask "was your daddy a diabetic? Anybody in your family have a history of cancer? Anybody have a history of glaucoma?" Doctors know that DNA is strong and transferable. I hate those questionnaires. I understand the need for them but I want to answer "no" on all of them *(not recommending you do this)*. I want to answer "no" because I confess that the curse is broken. I have a new DNA. I've been adopted! I'm no longer in fear of bondage, but God the Father has adopted me!

Romans 8:15 For you did not receive the spirit of bondage again to fear, but you received the Spirit of adoption by whom we cry out, "Abba, Father."

I got a new spiritual DNA running through these veins, and the doctors can't even explain it. It's like Superman DNA, its Jesus' DNA.

Doctors know that DNA is transferable and strong in the natural. Dear brothers and sisters, it's just as strong in the spiritual. Satan has assigned demons that have been studying your family for generations. That is how a kid can grow up and never be with their mom and dad but still possess traits like their mom and dad. You may call that "odd," but in all reality it is spiritual.

It's a spiritual thing to see how

generational curses and blessings can be passed down even though you don't know the people. My daughter is so funny. She will do things like her cousins, and she's never with her cousins. She acts like her cousins and possesses traits like them and yet she's never around them. But that bloodline is strong! DNA is strong! Spiritual DNA is just as strong.

What your family did around you became normal to you. I used to think "don't talk about my family. I can talk about my sister, but you can't talk about my sister or else we will be fighting." If you're anything like me, it was normal to defend your family's mess. There's no place like home because that's familiar to us, isn't it? But if you want to be free from the ungodly traits in your family, the first step is acknowledging them to the Father.

What you thought growing up as normal may have been anti-bible. Some things to some of us are just what we do because that's how we were raised; they're familiar to us.

In First and Second Samuel, there was a prophet by the name of Samuel. He anointed Saul to become King. Saul disobeyed what God tells him to do. Samuel dies, and Saul disobeyed God. The Bible says an "evil spirit came to torment him." Saul didn't know what to do when he no longer had his prophetic voice to give him instructions. Samuel was that voice to him, and Samuel had died.

Saul then called for the Witch of Endor. The witch came into Saul's house and said, "What can I do for you Saul," and Saul asks, "Would you please summon the spirit of Samuel."

Now I have to educate you because some of you think and believe in ghosts and you're a Christian. There are no such things as ghosts. Demon spirits yes, but ghosts of people who have died, no. Let me fix dysfunctional theology. When people die, they are gone. Here's what the Bible says:

2 Corinthians 5:8 …to be absent from the body and to be present with the Lord.

Whether you are saved or not, you're going to leave this earth and stand before the judge. Now then, the question arises, if the Witch of Endor summoned Samuel's spirit, what and who did she summon? I believe she summoned a familiar spirit. The word familiar originates from the word "Familia" which means family. She summoned the spirit that knew Samuel's generations. She summoned the demon spirit that knew how to imitate Samuel's ancestry.

Satan has sent out demonic agents throughout generations to learn your family. The family you didn't even know and was never around. He has sent spirits through the generations to study those before you to curse the generations to come and stop the blessing from flowing. Now, *that familiar thing is what you bend to*. A familiar spirit imitates your ancestry and knows them and you better than yourself. Knows what you like, what you have a *"taste"* for. Knows how to pressure you to give in. Knows how to get to you. Knows how to work you, knows how to trick you, knows how to lie to you, and knows how to suck the faith out of you; because generational curses are spiritual!

These demonic spirits want you to repeat the cycle of your forefathers, so you don't get free and activate the blessing. They want you to be an abuser because abuse is what is common and familiar in your family. They want you to manipulate because you got manipulated as a child. They want you to be broke and live in poverty because you lived in poverty, and disfunction growing up. It's a familiar spirit that attaches to a family that brings curses upon generations to come.

These "traits" have been passed down from demonic principalities and are now viewed as "normalcy." We say things like "that's how our family did it, done it, and does it" or "It is what I know and am used to" or; "it is just normal to us."

Don't say things like "he's going to be just like his daddy." I don't want my daughter being just like her daddy because there are things in my past I hate that haunts me still to this day. It's a spiritual issue, and I am gauging her spirit! I guard her and watch over her. This is why she doesn't go to people's houses. She isn't being watched by just anybody. I don't throw her from one house to another. I'm guarding her against the generational bends that are familiar to my blood line. I'm wise as a serpent. I'm looking; I'm watching. We tell our daughter, not to sit on anybody's lap; I don't care if they're a cousin, a uncle or a friend of the family because I know what's familiar and the curse has been broken.

My dad had a father; his name was Emmanuel from Mexico City. My grandfather met his wife and had my daddy, Gilbert. After my father was born, my grandfather left my father. My father at the age of sixteen went to find Emmanuel. My dad knocked on his dad's door, and my grandfather came to the door and said: "Who are you?" My dad said: "I'm your son and I want to have a relationship with you." My grandfather pulled out a gun and shot him and told him never to come back again. My mother and my father met in Evergreen Colorado, at Teen Challenge, (which is a drug rehabilitation facility). They were just nineteen years of age. They got married and moved to Omaha, Nebraska. They had my sister, and fourteen months later I was born. When my mom had me, my dad left our family. I never saw him again. When I went to find him, I found out he committed suicide and was no longer alive. Many years later, my wife and I were in a meeting, and a false prophet pulled me out and told me "in ten years the curses of your father will be passed on and you will see the manifestation in your life try to haunt and plague you, but if you fight you will win." I said "the devil is a liar" and I immediately denounced the false word into the atmosphere.

I broke that curse a long time ago and made a declaration to the Lord "I will be a good daddy when I have children. I am going to love my children when I have kids, and I refuse to leave them. I'm going to be around! I'm going to take them places and make the best memories." I take my little girl on daddy-daughter dates all the time, and she'll let you know all about it. She will tell me "Hey Dad, I think it's time for a date." She told me on a recent date that she doesn't want a husband when she grows up because she's going to marry me. I have broken the curse and so can you!

Generational curses have or are currently operating in your life. I want to give you the ammunition to break them. First thing's first; ACKNOWLEDGE IT!

You need to set some alone time to be still before the Lord. During this time you should not throw your family under the bus, per say. Do not demean or disrespect your forefathers or parents, but between you and the Lord, be honest. Be honest with you and Jesus.

Remember you have to honor

them! This is not a time to bash anyone or disrespect those who have paved good roads in your life along with the bad. It's not your job to be mean-spirited when you're on the journey to freedom. And don't do it in a demeaning or a disrespectful way. But what I'm about to show is what I did. I sat down with a pen and notepad. I looked at both sides of my family. I then made a list. On one side of the list, I listed all the good traits; on another, I listed all the bad traits and struggles that didn't line up with the Word of God. I then, one by one, read the traits out loud and acknowledged that those traits were working in me. I then repented of them and asked God to forgive me, and loose me from the traits of a physical and spiritual bloodline that didn't please Him. There is something powerful when you write them out and see them, then read them out loud for your ears to hear them. You will feel a weight lifted off of you when you confess them to the Lord.

There are times after this you will see them rise and try to manifest through you. When that happens, be quick to acknowledge them to the Lord and ask for immediate forgiveness.

I also want to encourage you to keep these things between you and the Lord alone. You don't need to discuss them with others, for that would be gossip, and you can harm the people you love. Acknowledge them before the Lord and begin your steps to freedom.

CHAPTER 9
STEPS TO FREEDOM

Now you have acknowledged these things to the Lord, and the Lord alone. You have confessed them and asked Him to forgive you for manifesting these in your life. Now let's look into the following steps that will empower you to walk in freedom and deliverance from generational curses.

1. ACKNOWLEDGE IT.

2. GET A SCRIPTURAL FOUNDATION.

A good place to start is Galatians 3:13-14. Confess it, read it, memorize it, get it in your heart! The Word is the standard, the fuel by which freedom flows.

3. COMMIT YOURSELF TO OBEYING THE WORD.

Don't just read the Word but obey it. Deuteronomy 28 teaches that if we want the blessing to come and the curse to go, we must obey the Word of God. Do you want poverty broken off your money? Then you need to obey what God said to do with your money. What does it say? Dig in the Word and discover. Then obey it.

4. CONFESS YOUR FAITH IN JESUS AS LORD.

Allow Jesus to Lord you, not just save you. When He is Lord you walk in obedience to the Holy Spirit. If Jesus is not Lord of every area of your life, then He is not Lord of any of your life. He is

God! He isn't looking to be just an opportunity in your back pocket to be used only when you need something. Freedom will not remain if that is your mindset. He isn't Lord if He is your "wing man" or "co-pilot." He wants to be your Leader, your King, your Master, your Lord. When He is the Lord of your life Satan flees. Surrender your heart fully to Jesus and allow him to Lord you.

5. ACKNOWLEDGE THE INIQUITY THAT WORKS THROUGH YOU AND YOUR FAMILY'S ANCESTRY.

You've got to acknowledge the specific iniquity. You are not guilty of your family's sins, but they do affect you. It is imperative you confess the sins of those who lived before you out loud. You are addressing the spiritual realm and letting every demon know you are stopping the curse.

6. FORGIVE OTHERS OF THEIR SHORTCOMINGS.

I hear you, "Come on Pastor, how do I do that? How can I let this pain go? You don't know what they did to me or how deeply they wounded me." I don't, you are right, but ask Jesus to help you. He will empower you to forgive others, supernaturally! Lean upon Jesus and ask him to help you.

7. DENOUNCE ALL CONTACT WITH THE OCCULT.

Many have said to me "Pastor, I'm not worshipping the devil! I don't pray to the dark world in the center of a pentagram." That may be true, but many of you watch movies and partake in media that does. You listen to music that is the antithesis of biblical doctrine. Many of you entertain yourself through media that pushes sorcery, witchcraft, magical arts, perversion, palm reading, yoga classes that put you in a "meditative state." All of these are examples and doors to the spiritual world. Any type of horror films or movies and the like, have been birthed out of the occult. Who do you think gives producers the ideas for horror movies? Why do you think horror movies are so dark? God didn't give them those ideas; they came from a DARK place. The Holy Ghost would NEVER give a person an idea to make a movie about cutting off a man's head and putting it in a freezer. If the Holy Ghost didn't implant that thought, there is only one other option. Get the junk out of your house and rid your home and mind of all occult tools and practices. You can't have freedom and keep trash in your mind. Get it out!

Throw away horoscope readings and your daily future Facebook life reading. That's all the occult! If you've got the Book of Mormon in your house, throw it away.

Revelation 22:18 For I testify to everyone who hears the words of the prophecy of this book: If anyone adds to these things, God will add to him the plagues (curses) that are written in this book

Get the Buddha statues and voodoo decorations out of your

house and throw them away.

Stop practicing out-of-body meditation, the seeking of miracles, the fundamentals of yoga. I don't practice yoga because I'm a Christian and the fundamentals of it came from mysticism. Now again, please hear me. If you've been doing it, there is no shame, and I am not trying to beat you down but usher in freedom.

And please for the love of God, throw the books away that contain the teachings of karma.

If you want to be free and stay free, these six steps are a must!!!

CLOSING PRAYER

As we come to a close to this book, I want you to repeat the following prayer out loud: *"Heavenly Father, I come before you today in the name of Jesus Christ my Lord. I denounce all generational curses that have been handed down from generations past. Free me from the chains that bind me. Free me from the traits that my bloodline leans and bends toward. Show me the things I do that are contrary to the Word so I can repent of them. Satan, the blood of Jesus be against you and all your tactics. God, enable me to forgive and let go of things that have hindered and hurt me. Your Kingdom come, and may your will be done in my life. I give heaven permission to break out in my life and for victory to be my testimony. Bless my parents and grandparents and all those who were before me (if still living). Help me to honor them and teach my children the principle of honor. In the matchless name of Jesus Christ my Lord, Amen."*

ABOUT THE AUTHOR

Through obscurity, abandonment, and rejection a Man of God was birthed. Pastor Brian Gallardo grew up in a home without his father. He found out later in life that his father had committed suicide. He grew up in addiction and poverty which oppressed his family. Pastor Brian Gallardo beat the odds and is a perfect testimony that God can take a mess and turn it into a miracle.

Pastor Gallardo graduated from Valor Christian College before moving to Omaha, Nebraska in 1999. There, he served as a pastoral assistant under Pastor James K. Hart at Eagles Nest Worship Center for ten years. With their pastor's blessing, in 2008, Pastors Brian and Jillian Gallardo moved to Missouri and started Lifegate Church.

Pastor Gallardo has appeared on The Word Network, Juice TV, TBN Salsa and TBN with the following great men and women of God: Pastor Rod Parsley, Pastor Jonathan Miller, Pastor Tony Suarez, Pastor Matt Austin, Dr. Lee Stroble, Dr. Medina Pullings, Bishop Michael Pitts, Ashton Parsley, and many others. His TV Program, Invasion TV, airs weekly on TBN Salsa.

Together with his wife and family, they desire to *reach* the world for Jesus, *build* and strengthen the body of Christ, and without restraint serve and *pursue* Jesus until He comes again.

For more information about Pastor Brian Gallardo, or to book him at your next conference, please visit:

- www.briangallardo.com
- Twitter: briangallardo
- Instagram: pastorbgallardo
- Facebook: Pastor Brian Gallardo

Made in the USA
Coppell, TX
22 May 2020

26231618R00089